Mackenzie Bell

Pictures of Travel and other Poems

Vol. 2

Mackenzie Bell

Pictures of Travel and other Poems
Vol. 2

ISBN/EAN: 9783337292898

Printed in Europe, USA, Canada, Australia, Japan

Cover: Foto ©Thomas Meinert / pixelio.de

More available books at **www.hansebooks.com**

Pictures of Travel

And Other Poems

Pictures of Travel

And Other Poems

By

Mackenzie Bell

Author of

" Spring's Immortality and other Poems "
" Charles Whitehead : A Biographical and Critical Monograph "
" Christina Rossetti : A Biographical and Critical Study "
&c.

WITH SIX ILLUSTRATIONS

Boston
Little, Brown, & Co.
1898

University Press
John Wilson & Son, Cambridge, U. S. A.

TO

WILLIAM MACDONALD SINCLAIR

ARCHDEACON OF LONDON

IN MEMORY OF MANY HAPPY HOURS

SPENT AT THE CHAPTER HOUSE

ST. PAUL'S CATHEDRAL

Prefatory Note

I AM obliged to the editors of "The Pall Mall Magazine," " The Churchman," London, "Black and White," London, " The Lady's Realm," London, " The Literary World," London, and other periodicals, for permission to include in this volume poems which originally appeared in their pages, and to Messrs. Hutchinson & Co. for their courtesy in allowing me to include the two sonnets, "To a Lady Playing the Harp in her Chamber," which were first published in the third series of " The Savage Club Papers."

In stanza V. of " The Battle's Pause," one of the poems in this volume, an attempt is made to paint a picture of what in other times was very familiar in the estuary of the Mersey — the sailing out of many merchantmen which had long been wind-bound. This must indeed have been a singularly beautiful sight as viewed from such a coign of vantage, for example, as Seacombe beach opposite

PREFATORY NOTE

to Liverpool. What marine spectacle in these days of steam can equal in picturesqueness the sailing-ships of the early part of the century, imposing in their proportions, and moving majestically through the water under favouring conditions? With reference to other lines in the same stanza it may be mentioned that St. Nicholas, the ancient parish church of Liverpool, is near the river, and is a noticeable object from it, and that in the early part of 1814 there was an extraordinarily severe frost in the neighbourhood of Liverpool with ice-floes on the Mersey.

"A Plea for Faith" was written, and its title chosen, before I read, both in manuscript and in proof, my friend Dr. George S. Keith's treatise, "A Plea for a Simpler Faith." "A Plea for a Simpler Faith" was not suggested by my poem.

MACKENZIE BELL.

LONDON, *September 1898.*

Contents

[1] For the first series of " Pictures of Travel," see the author's previous volume, " Spring's Immortality and Other Poems " (third edition, 1896).

CONTENTS

MISCELLANEOUS POEMS

RELIGIOUS POEMS

List of Illustrations

PICTURES OF TRAVEL

SECOND SERIES

After Sunset off Pauillac

(*Gironde*)

THE day is gone, but yonder fading streaks

    Of light still fleck the bosom of the sky.

Swart Night comes swiftly.   Hark, that sound

       bespeaks

    My nearness to the ocean, 't is the cry

Of some belated sea-bird, and I hear

    The ripples at my feet.   A low sweet song

Monotonous, yet musical and clear,

    Is breeze-borne from a vessel's deck along.

The crew raise anchor quickly, and away

    She glides into the gloom, while growing low

And ever lower sounds the roundelay.

What now may be her fortune none can know.

Like her, o'er Life's strange, trackless sea we

sail,

Nor know if calm or tempest will prevail.

Evening in the Forest of Meudon

(*Seine et Oise*)

RETURNING sometimes from the fields of sleep,

   I seem to see that twilight once again,

That twilight as mysterious, rich, and deep,

   As yonder blackbird's strain.

I see the sombre loveliness around;

   I feel the sense of awe, the enthralling peace,

Of Nature's woodland silence, for no sound

   Makes here that silence cease.

Anon I see the waters of the lake

 Gleam in the last hues of the sunset glow,

While here and there the lazy cattle slake

 Their thirst, and homeward go.

But hear, O hear that sudden burst of song,

 At last it is the full-voiced nightingales!

While mellow cuckoos sing, and so prolong

 Music as daylight fails.

 * * * * * * * * *

Long hours have passed, and man and beast and

  bird

 Rest; yet my heart is filled with pure delight,

And lo, a single nightingale is heard

 Amid the moonless night.

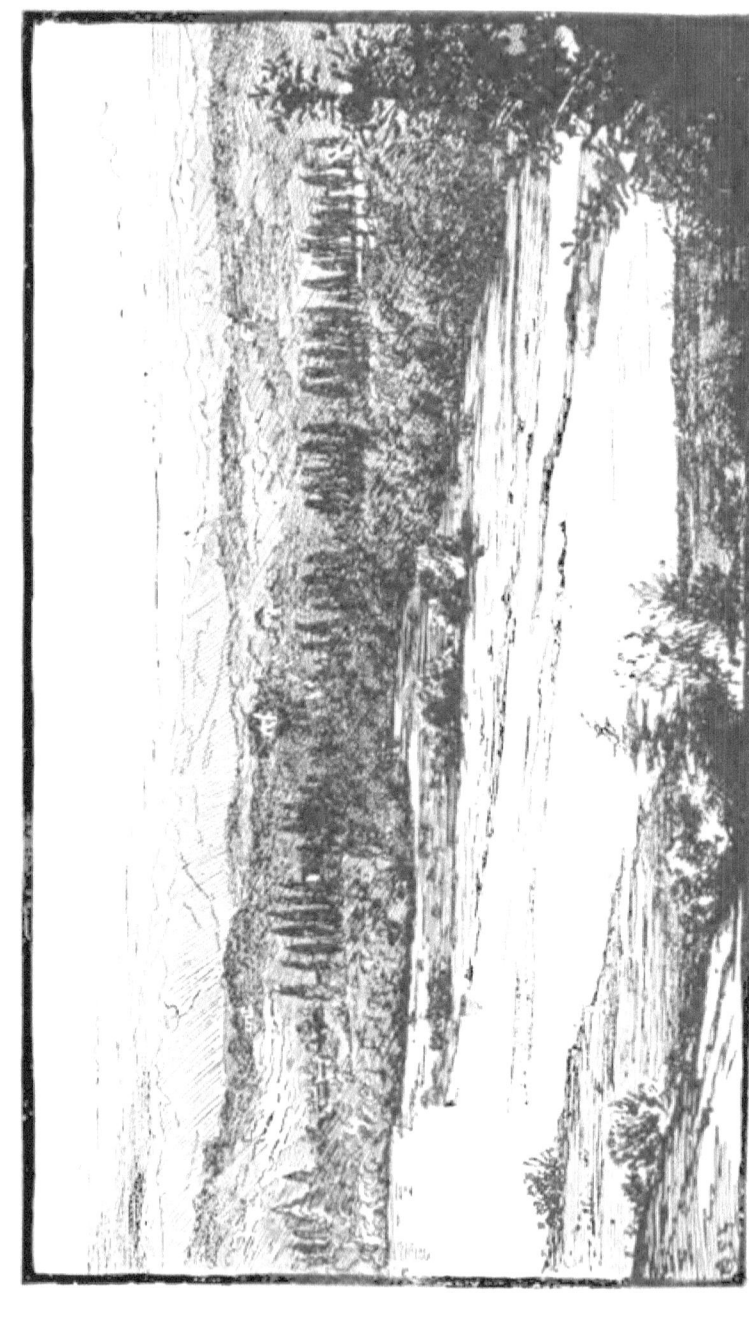

Wild Roses and Snow

(Basses Pyrénées)

How sweet the sight of roses

    In English lanes of June,

When every flower uncloses

    To meet the kiss of noon.

How strange the sight of roses —

    Roses both sweet and wild —

Seen where a valley closes

    'Mid mountain heights up-piled.

Wild Roses and Snow

Upon whose sides remaining

   Is strewn the purest snow,

By its chill power restraining

   The tide of Spring's soft glow.

Yet God who gave the pureness

   To yon fair mountain snow,

Gives also the secureness

   Whereby these roses blow.

At Sea —Off the Mouth of the Garonne —Sunset

A TWILIT halo gilds the troubled sky,

And gilds the heaving waters far and nigh;

About me here is some strange loveliness

Which, as the shadows deepen, grows not less.

Hark! Now, not once or twice, but o'er and o'er,

In solemn grandeur comes the deep-voiced roar

Of strong Atlantic surges; where I stand

I look, but see no welcome speck of land.

How beautiful is yonder distant sail

Illumined yet; but soon my eyes must fail

To trace its further course, for it will be

Lost in the glory of the sunset sea.

And as I gaze, and gaze, dim thoughts arise —

Thoughts of Man's destiny; these callous skies

Seem types of earthly cruelty, and now

The sea, like man, is sad — I know not how.

The air is still; no wingéd wanderer cleaves

The silence in his flight, as Night receives

Ere long her stately queen the crescent moon,

Whose glimmering beams show all the billows

soon.

"Nature is great, and Man is impotent." — *p.* 11.

Near St. Sauveur

(Hautes Pyrénées)

Lo, what a glorious prospect is revealed —

Mountains and snow, and pine-trees beauty-clad!

Upon the sloping sides of monarch heights

Reposes gracefully a misty veil,

In wreaths almost transparent; but ev'n now

Its mass divides, and clear against the sky

Rises each giant summit, calm and grand,

Proud that its lone, its vast, its God-wrought

    strength

Defies so long decay. I needs must feel

Nature is great, and Man is impotent,

Yet still how much his art hath made increase

To this rare store of beauty.   Each small patch

Perceived upon the mountain side, reclaimed

From barren wilderness, what power it hath

To cheer the eye.   To me it often seems

As though no prospect reached perfection till

It showed some kindly trace of human toil.

" . . . waters of the waveless lake." — *p.* 13

On the Lake of Geneva

A SILVERN haze is over all.   At hand

Are gently swaying poplars, rippling larches,

And firmly rooted firs, while further off

Gleam azure waters of the waveless lake.

Beyond again are mountains; not, as oft,

Gaunt snow-capped monarch peaks, but bright

    with verdure.

The rocks throw shadows quaint upon the grass;

White *chalets* peep among the clustering vines;

Gay boats glide smoothly on with placid sails

Widely outspread.

THE BATTLE'S PAUSE

The Battle's Pause

(An Imaginary Episode at Waterloo)

I

At daybreak on a lonely sea

Strange is the silence; heavily

The louring clouds loom dim and dun,

Till comes at length the far-off sun;

Strange is the silence of the day

Where waves are hushed in some fair bay;

Strange is the silence of the night

Where throned in space the stars give light;

Strange is the silence that ofttimes

Broods o'er the city's shame and crimes;

Strange is the silence of the room

Where lingering sickness hangs in gloom;

Strange is the silence after death

Where anguished sound departs with breath;

But stranger is the silence when

The moans are stilled of wounded men,

Where stilled an instant are the cries

That from wild scenes of strife arise

As noise of rapid volleys cease, —

As God grants here and there release, —

As suddenly the senses yield

To silence on the battle-field.

II

In these fleet moments interposed

Ere yet once more the foemen closed,

In inner vision every man

Lived o'er again his whole life's span.

Only of plunder many thought,

But here and there was one who caught

Swift glimpses, borne on spirit-wings,

Of God, of Heaven, of holy things —

Who felt his courage no less high

Because he was prepared to die.

III

One dreams of his betrothed in France,

A dark-eyed girl with laughing glance,

And wonders if he soon shall meet

Her tender looks, her smile so sweet.

"Ah, ma Lucille," with tears he cries,

"Fain would I see the glad surprise

Break the calm gaze of your dear eyes,

As with high hope I come once more,

Unwounded from the field of war.

Fain would I see your rippling curls,

More precious than those lustrous pearls,

My gift to you — that sometimes deck

The stately beauty of your neck —

That on your bosom rise and fall,

White rivals of its whiteness, all

Eclipsed in utter loveliness.

Fain would I see again that dress;

Its dainty hue of mellow brown

Sets off the clustering curls that crown

Your shapely head.   Fain would I see

The happy village revelry

That joyous day which makes you mine —

When underneath the ancient vine

Around Saint Etienne's porch we pass

Just coming from the wedding Mass,

And leaving near to the altar stair

The *curé* with his silvery hair,

Low kneeling now in holy prayer,

To crave a blessing on us there,

His guileless, gladsome, saintly soul

As spotless as his pure white stole."

IV

Another soldier sees a room

O'ershadowed by a partial gloom,

As heavy curtains shade the light

From a wan sufferer's weakened sight,

And on a couch is seen a boy,

Whose wasted face, all flushed with joy,

Looks on a portrait, newly there,

Of a tall youth with raven hair,

Clad in a garb of martial hue.

And then in accents heartfelt, true,

He speaks the words: "Would that I too

With my dear brother still could be

Where Valour leads to Victory."

V

A Scotsman here among "The Greys"

Chafes inly now at war's delays, —

Would but the bugle sound the charge!

Would that he were once more at large

Among the flying cuirassiers!

He knows no pity, knows no fears, —

For him each instant passes slow

Passed not in fight against the foe,--

'T is hard to stand, nor give one blow —

It suits his fiery humour ill

To be a living target still,

Nor use his good sword at his will.

Near him " The Inniskillings " share

A post of danger — everywhere

Brave soldiers they, — who greatly dare.

VI

Before an English soldier lie

Down-trodden fields of wheat and rye,

But his tired vision does not meet

These blood-stained fields of rye and wheat.

He sees not how his comrades here
Reveal no sign of craven fear;
While they with bandaged hand or face,
Still struggle on, nor quit their place.
He sees not, as in many rifts
The smoke of battle, rising, lifts,
How everywhere all undismayed
Still firm they stand as on parade,
Although their thinning ranks disclose
How hard with them the conflict goes.
He sees the Mersey; fresh and cool
The east wind blows from Liverpool
To Seacombe beach, where, loitering,
He stood one early morn of spring
A month or two before. The day
At first had seemed but chill and grey,

Till brilliant sunshine suddenly

Had flooded all the estuary.

For weeks the west wind had prevailed —

No ship, if outward bound, had sailed;

But now the fickle wind had veered,

And now the sailors' hearts were cheered,

While a whole fleet — a gallant show

Of eager ships — was free to go.

Full many a vessel, towards the bar

Across the waters near and far,

Moves buoyantly.   With what delight

He looks upon the goodly sight

Of canvas spread to catch the breeze

That dances o'er the rippling seas!

How shapely are the skiffs which pass

Between him and St. Nicholas!

How graceful is the distant town,

Which gaily o'er the waves looks down!

Changed is the scene since 'mid the snow

He saw it scarce a year ago.

Then many a white and large ice-floe

Reared its strange shape on every side,

While tossing idly on the tide.

VII

Another soldier sees his home

Where whirls the wild Biscayan foam;

Where surges beat with sullen roar

Upon a dreary pine-clad shore.

There his good mother yet must wait

For many a month disconsolate,

Waiting, still waiting for her child,

With heavy heart unreconciled

To his long absence — her distress

At times most pitiful to guess.

He sees her in her peasant's dress

At household duties, at her door

At eve and morning, evermore

Thinking with heavy heart of him;

With unshed tears her eyes grow dim,

Looking, aye looking constantly,

Across the same sad, dreary sea.

Again he hears the gleeful noise

And chatter of the village boys,

He even hears the sound once more

Of *sabots* on a cottage floor.

Again it seems that mournful day

When he, alas, was called away;

Again he sees the fishing-boat

    That comes to bear him to the town;

Again his home grows more remote

    As o'er the sea the sun goes down.

Still he beholds his mother's face,

And still he feels her warm embrace,

He knows her anguished doubts, her fears,

And would-be smiles, he feels her tears.

He hears the heaving waters nigh —

He sees above, an angry sky,

Dark, yet with streaks of mingled grey,

Fading while swiftly dies the day.

He passes to the gathering gloom

As though to some impending doom;

Drear seems the earth, the sky, the main —

He feels that Nature knows his pain.

" . . . a crag-perched village. " —p. 29.

VIII

A youthful soldier looked around

Upon the ghastly battle ground.

He was a conscript, ne'er before

Had he beheld the face of War,

He saw not all its deeps of pain,

For former scenes arose again.

Once more he was a child at play,

In that steep village street which lay,

Crag-perched, 'mid tree-boles gnarled and grey

With age.   It was the close of day.

Was that the church he knew of old,

That the rude cross where he was told

The story of the ancient time

So full of mystery, lust, and crime?

Ah, how he loved yon olive wood,

To him how sweet its solitude,

How oft on many a summer night

He watched from there the fading light,

Till grew more bright and yet more bright

The distant lamps of great Marseilles,

And when at length the daylight fails,

Fair seem the stars, fair seems the sea,

Ah, how at once his memory

Brings back for him these moonlit hours

'Mid fragrance of the orange flowers.

Fresh is the air, and soft and still,

Save when the *mistral* brings its chill.

Once more he feels the morning breeze

Which gently curls the azure seas

Around his father's fishing-boat,

That like a live thing seems to float.

Lovely it looks with dark brown sail,

Outspread to catch each gentle gale.

And when the noontide comes at length

The crew refresh their waning strength

By frugal meal, or merry jest,

By games, or cheerful talk, or rest.

One man had fought where waned the star

Of France in fight off Trafalgar;

Another speaks of Austerlitz,

And shows the combat as he sits.

With eager words, with eyes aflame,

He tells the tale, "The Emperor came

To our right flank when sore distressed:

We needed succour, needed rest,

Yet better was his presence then

Than of a thousand untired men."

So, early stirred the martial fire

In the boy's breast — the proud desire

To win the soldier's honoured name,

To win the soldier's meed of fame.

To him an order comes ere long

To join the army; 'mid a throng

Of youths he gains a barrack square,

Strange seems the ceaseless bustle there.

Here well-groomed horses drink their fill;

Here is an active squad at drill;

Here words of gaiety he hears;

And here a mother stands in tears;

Here stands a veteran hale, erect,

In garb that points to no neglect,

Though he has marched full many a mile,

In blazing sunshine all the while,

A faultless soldier he has been,

No chance of war can change his mien.

Here stands a youth with shambling gait,

In soldier's dress, yet unelate,

With stupid look, and vacant face,

As though his garb were some disgrace;

Here, agile gunners clean a gun;

And here, his day's work nearly done,

A driver of the army train

Brings in his store of food and grain.

The conscript thinks with what glad heart

In scenes like these he took a part.

With joy his boy's heart overflows,

He longs to smite his country's foes,

Of what he leaves he scarce takes heed,

Civilian clothes he doffs with speed,

To him his uniform brings life,

He thinks of glory in the strife.

He thinks, as now the sun goes down,

Of lasting honour and renown;

To him War is not sad, but strange —

It gives him motion, stir, and change.

*   *   *   *   *   *   *   *

Through all the long, the happy marches

   Across Provence, now bright with spring,

He sees the gay triumphal arches,

   He hears once more the joy-bells ring.

And then one day, through beat of drums,

He hears the cry, "The Emperor comes,"

"The Emperor comes" — on every side

They pass the word with looks of pride.

Each soldier feels his courage rise,

Fresh pleasure sparkles in his eyes,

And while he stands the more upright,

Sees his accoutrements are bright,

And hopes his bayonet, sword, or lance

Will seem to that all-piercing glance

As sword or bayonet ought to look.

For who could bear the sharp rebuke

Or face his comrades' words or jeers,

Or worse, his comrades' covert sneers,

At one the Emperor deigned to chide?

An hour has gone; the corps espied

The staff approaching, near a wood

It stood to arms.   Kind Nature's mood

Was peaceful: there the stock-dove coo'd;

The dreamer sees one purple flower,

Which decked the spot that sunny hour.

"The Emperor is an altered man

Since Leipsic," says a veteran.

And yet the great Napoleon seems

The ideal of a soldier's dreams,

As now he passes on his course,

Erect upon his snow-white horse

Amid his marshals.   Soult and Ney,

Heroes of many a well-fought day,

Ride near him now, in gayest trim.

They jest, and sometimes speak with him —

Yet never seem to lose the sense

Of that strange man's strange influence —

Of that magnetic, cruel power

By which Napoleon, hour by hour,

Until his fiery race was run,

Remorselessly swayed every one.

Firm are his lips, stern are his eyes —

Hard eyes, where naught of gladness lies;

Yet signs there are of wasting life,

Wasting through care and lust of strife,

That drooping lip, that haggard cheek,

Of pain, of ebbing force, they speak.

But none, save veterans here and there,

Perceive his chill, his altered air;

The troops, o'erjoyed to see his face,

See in his glance a sign of grace:

His presence cures their every ill,

And "Vive l'Empereur!" their shout is still.

IX

A tranquil, sunlit village green

Sees one young Englishman: between

A row of elms he catches sight

Of one dear cottage; to the right

Lies the grey rectory, and beyond

Old Farmer Granger's ricks and pond,

Just where the high road quickly dips.

Here as a child he sailed his ships,

While loafers from the alehouse near

Gladdened his heart by words of cheer,

And showed him how to set his sail,

To woo the soft, the favouring gale.

*   *   *   *   *   *   *

He sees again the long sea beach

A mile or two from home; the reach

" . . . the reach
The farm-folk call the Little Broad." — p. 65.

The farm-folk called the Little Broad

Gleams in the sun, while boys applaud

His feats of strength; or on the sea

Perchance he rows right merrily,

While myriad skylarks, singing, soar

Above the sand cliffs on the shore;

Or looking seaward from the land

He views the sunset vague and grand.

X

A Frenchman thinks with many a fear

Of his one sister — very dear

Is she to him, a girl most fair.

He sees e'en now her dark-brown hair,

And inly speaks, "Herself a flower

She hawks sweet blossoms hour by hour

Through many a parched Parisian street,

Gladly, though oft with toil-worn feet.

'T is she who wins the daily bread

And shelter for my father's head,

Since age and sickness disallow

Him strength to earn his living now;

While *I*, who should have been their stay,

Without appeal am forced away,

Simply because some men — whose aims

I do not know and scarce their names —

Have fixedly resolved on War.

And **I** — one of their human store —

Am made to face death at their will

Till kings and emperors have their fill."

How strange are we! he who so dreamed

And all unpatriotic seemed,

When fierce again began the strife,

Fought with the best — cared not for life.

The vision changes, and he sees

The comely, the belovèd trees

That droop in summer's sultry blaze

Along the white Parisian ways.

In one old street he sees a spot

Shaded by lime-trees: there is not

A cooler nook, and side by side

An old man and a maid abide

In sweet affectionate converse there,

To rest, to breathe its fresher air.

'T is those he loves, and for a space

He treads himself that well-known place,

So keen his inner sight.   And soon

His sister starts through afternoon

Long hours, and near the Tuileries

She stays, then moves along the quays,

She is so fair, so pure, so sweet,

She seems to gladden all the street.

And many look at her, and smile;

They note her brave looks all the while,

They know her toil of every day,

Toil such as wears her youth away.

And one, an honest artisan,

A homely, upright, thrifty man,

Poring o'er some long-cherished plan,

Passing, thinks, "Would she were my wife,

Happy were I though hard my life."

And with a Frenchman's frugal care

He saves, and saving, dreams of her.

Although from childhood's earliest days

She knew the drear Parisian ways

(Gay to the rich, drear to the poor),

From every harm she walks secure,

From virtue none her steps allure.

In thought, in actions, she is good,

Kindness her constant habitude.

She raises soft and pleading eyes

With something of a chaste surprise

At many a word, at many a sight,

That comes to her by day or night.

All innocence without, within,

She sees, yet sees not all their sin.

XI

Thus runs each hapless soldier's dream

In that short pause — that restful gleam

Of blesséd peace.

                  But, hark, there comes

The gathering roll of distant drums

Beating the charge, and then the sound

Of musketry.   Men gaze around

Half in surprise — then hear again

The clash of arms, the cry of pain,

The wounded horse's neigh; and so

Fateful with pain the gaunt hours go.

TO A WORKER AMONG THE
POOR

To a Worker among the Poor

COURAGE like yours has still a mighty power

To purify the mind from hour to hour,

To permeate with thrilling force the soul,

To give new confidence, new self-control,

To make each faulty faculty so clear

That, though you plainly see the danger near,

You scorn to dread it — scorn to turn aside,

Duty your first, your chief, your only guide.

The soldier 'mid the scenes of deadly strife

Thinks of his country — thinks not of his life;

And shall we then in these degenerate days

Speak of him lightly, cease to give him praise?

Yet Glory has for him her ancient charm,

Excitement nerves for him his stalwart arm;

When bullets whistle in the dread advance,

For him there comes the touch of old Romance.

War has its use: sometimes it keeps alive

Those qualities that make a nation thrive;

In certain minds it checks the love of self;

It teaches self-control, and scorn of pelf;

Once and again it seems to make for good,

By teaching patriotism and fortitude

That love of country flippant scribes deride

As but a foible — but a foolish pride —

That love of country which a nation's fame

Exalts, whose absence brings a nation's shame.

Yet War, alas! not seldom seems to be

Only a form of licensed butchery —

One of the ills that from our passions spring —

The warrior's courage but a puny thing.

Yes; yours is truer courage, for it comes

Not from the fife's shrill note, nor roll of drums,

Not from the maddening energy of pain

Where Horror, heedless, stalks among the slain,

But from that hidden strength which has its

     birth

In some sublimer sphere beyond this earth.

That bravery is not yours which men acclaim,

That bravery is not yours which gives men fame,

Yours is the courage which but few suspect,

Yours is the courage which can bear neglect,

Yours is the courage which can suffer long,

The courage of the man whose soul is strong,

Who labours on, still doing silent good,

Nor stays his hand for Man's ingratitude.

Though oft you seem to till a thankless soil,

Your prayers are never vain, nor vain your toil;

Some fruit you yet may have to cheer your heart,

In some new epoch you may bear a part;

But ev'n if now, through your short span of years

Your work be weary, and no fruit appears, —

Though, in humility, you look within,

Deeming your failure the result of sin, —

It is not so; for still our Father knows

What each requires — on each He still bestows

The discipline most needed; still He weighs

Our work with Heavenly scales; our purblind gaze

Finds failure often where He knows success.

All are His instruments, and so the less

His need of one man for the world's great need;

Righteous He is, to all He gives their meed

Of praise or blame; yet not like us He scans —

We see results, by them we make our plans,

And trust or trust not men.   Men's character

He reads with searching glance that cannot err,

And thinks not of results, but values still

Patience and faith, and will to do His will.

So to His best beloved oft gives He trial,

As to His Blesséd Son, of base denial,

And haply most will honour near His throne

Some humble follower by the world unknown.

Blurred is perspective by our earthly view —

To God perspective aye is clear and true.

Effort like yours ever to do the right

Will raise your soul from height to nobler height,

And gives at last that guerdon, full, unpriced,

The " Well done " of your life-long master, Christ.

A PLEA FOR FAITH

A Plea for Faith

LIFE! How mysterious does it seem, how strange

Its grief, its happiness, its shame, its sin —

How hard its changes are! Can we believe

In a great God of kindness infinite

Who yet can daily leave His hapless world

To be — for so it seems — the home of pain,

Pain often useless, often showered on those

Who seem to need it least? Can we believe

In Perfect Goodness and Omniscient Power

Permitting Evil to possess and spoil

His fair dominions, and to bring a curse —

An ageless and unceasing curse — upon them?

Alas, to our poor minds our futile years

Seem but a clueless maze.   When happiness

Is ours, a hidden canker-worm reveals

Its hateful presence, and too soon there comes

Something to vex the spirit, or to jar,

Something to cloud or check our perfect joy.

One man has buoyant health, and feels delight

In living merely, yet he finds how hard

Is poverty to bear; it oftentimes

Hangs round him as a changeless destiny.

Too rich is he to rank among the poor,

Too poor is he to rank among the rich;

Of neither class, he knows the ills of both.

Another man has ample wealth, and friends

Who love to do him honour, and to give

To him the zest in living which such friends

Alone can give.   Yet look!—alas, 't is clear

Disease's curse is on him, fell disease

For which weak human skill affords no cure

And scarce alleviation.   He is doomed

To pass a joyless life despite the joys

Surrounding him.

        Another man we see

With riches and with pulse of flawless health.

With steadfast, cheerful face he fronts the
    world,

And all seems well; yet could we look within,

Some grief we should perceive which saps his life

And makes it full of care — a grief that springs

Not from his fault; or oftentimes we see

Innocent children suffer for the sake

Of guilty parents, or a mother's heart

Guileless and pure, that bleeds for some loved son

Or daughter who, alas, has gone astray.

Not seldom in despondency we feel

As though the wrong is victor o'er the right,

As though our life were but a flake of foam

Cast by some cruel sea on some bleak shore,

A moment seen, and then for ever lost.

  And yet, if we deny that God exists

As perfect in His goodness as His power,

If we deny that Death, God's angel, brings

To man a nobler life, what do we gain

To compensate us for the hopes we lose?

For still we must endure the woes of life,

Still must we feel the longings which arise

For rest and peace amid our daily toil.

These we must still endure, and yet perceive

Beyond the grave no gleam of gathering light,

Nought save the gloom of nothingness before us.

But if we greet kind Faith, and let her hand

Lead us through all our years, though at the last

We find that hope of happier life is vain

(That 't were so would not change the argument)

Faith's guidance will have given a mighty boon

To us, in gladdening all our days on earth.

So even if we wholly set aside

Faith's fervent pleading with the intellect —

A pleading ever present, ever strong,

'T is wiser far to guide our minds to view

The problem still in some such wise as this,

'T is true amid our earthly life there runs

A tangled thread of strange perplexity

And much injustice; yet comes by and by

A nobler state of being, when that which seems

Unjust will be explained or set aright.

'Tis best to hold that there exists a God

Who made Man's mind with marvellous powers,
   though He

In His deep wisdom limited the scope

Of what He made, wherefore our reason's sphere

Of thought is swiftly reached, and so it seems

To us so frequently that human life

Hath such injustice in its fleeting years;

That He decrees that it is well for us

In humble trust to tread "the path of sorrow,"

Perchance as discipline for some high scheme

Of joy hereafter, or perchance to show

To others how the brave can conquer pain;

That Life's dark mysteries do but transcend,

Not contradict our reason, and when soon

Our earthly life shall close, there dawns a life

When He endows us with new gifts of mind.

Then chief among the pleasures it can give

Will be the thrill of joy when first we feel

That now we understand those mysteries

Which vexed our souls before — when first we find

That many "themes with which we cannot cope"

Grow clear, and "Earth's worst phrenzies" are at
    length

Forgotten in the joy of Hope's fruition.

MISCELLANEOUS POEMS

To ――

A Summer Evening in the Woods

I

How lovely are the woodland glades to-night,

The boughs slow moving in the balmy air,

As birds sing now and then from pure delight

With melody low-pitched, though scarce aware

They sing.   The branches erewhile gaunt and
   bare,

Have donned their daintiest dress; the insects
   keep

A dreamy revel, murmuring everywhere;

In these dear glades, so still, so dim, so deep,

Save for these lulling sounds kind Nature seems

    to sleep.

II

The voiceless stars shine out, and all too soon

The calm delicious summer twilight ends;

Yet but a little space, and lo! the moon

Has ris'n, and thence a flood of light descends,

While she amid the clouds, majestic, wends

Her queen-like way; obsequious stand they

    near,

Like courtiers round a throne; each object

    lends

Fresh beauty to the landscape made so clear

In this rare light that all its richer hues are here.

" . . . each object . . . made so clear
In this rare light." —p. 66.

III

Now in this evening walk there lives anew

That joyous summer evening long ago,

Sweet as to-night, when first I walked with

    you —

When, as the westering sun was sinking low,

I first knew all your love for me; and so

Each year since then more swiftly than the last

Has gone, for Time but made our love to grow.

Yes, while the years are hurrying to the past,

My one regret it is that still they fly so fast.

The Boy Chatterton to Himself

" Sublime of thought and confident of fame."

COLERIDGE, *Monody on the Death of Chatterton.*

THAT dotard soul I cannot comprehend,

Who knows no hope that, after many years

His name should be preserved by other means

Than by an entry in the parish books —

The soul who never knew the proud desire

To be remembered in far days unborn

By some great deed accomplished.

                            Therefore here

I make a vow — a vow unchanging, strong:

I will redeem the time, and, though the days

Are evil, yet it will be my delight

To toil unceasingly, that at the last

It shall be seen I have not lived in vain.

Men's hours are passed as sacred Scripture

    saith —

"They eat, they drink, are merry, and they die."

Few daily doings are of much account

In fifty years; then let my mind be set

On some fit theme meet for my noblest powers.

The Boy Coleridge to Himself

"O capacious soul!"

WORDSWORTH, *The Prelude, Book xiv.*

"I WONDER wherefore?" is the soul-stirred cry

Which wells up from the depths of human hearts

In every sphere of life — from lowly homes

And princely palaces — from hermit cells

And seething crowds — from youth and riper age

And longest length of years — from rich and

    poor —

From all who have the manliness to think —

In health or sickness — happiness or woe —

'Mid Life's supremest moments or its trifles

Which often make men ponder most.   And this

Incessant questioning is surely meant

As greatest food for hope — a token given

That, notwithstanding its abyss of sin,

Within man's soul the germs of good abide.

   Mysterious are the links that firmly weld

Our trains of thought together.   First we brood

On some small trivial matter — now the germ

Of musings somewhat loftier — then behold,

A thread is woven with our thought, and lo

It leads to higher themes ! — vast vistas new

For serious contemplation : — and we gain

Sublimest heights, as God-reflected thoughts

Transcending reason throng our kindled minds.

The Philosophy of our Feelings

'T is strange that what seems grief to-day

   Should seem like joy to-morrow,

That present bliss should pass away

   And seem, in future, sorrow.

Yet in the web of life we find,

   While its vague threads we measure,

The pattern of our mood of mind

   Traced out in pain or pleasure.

The Philosophy of Frequent Failure

In Youth's glad morning hours of strenuous life

Great contemplations often fill the mind

With noblest aspirations, while it seems

To us, as yet scarce touched by sordid care

And blighting prejudice, quite possible

Through our unaided strength to win at last

Some shining goal which glitters in our sight —

A goal which, when 't was won, would crown with

    good

The Universal Brotherhood of Man.

But as the years roll on we find the dream

Less easy of fulfilment, — for we feel

Our ardour less intense — our weary feet

Glide gently into that poor old-world groove

We so despised of yore, — and we are fain

To use fast-failing energy in strife

'Gainst daily troubles; higher aims forgotten.

Wind Fancies

MURMURING winds vague fancies carry
    To the heart while sweeping by,
And the fancies often tarry
    Though the winds that brought them die.

Now the fancies are of gladness,
    Life itself seems one delight;
Now the fancies are of sadness,
    Life itself seems dark as night.

To Frederick Tennyson

(*Died February* 26, 1898, *in his ninety-first year*)

ELDEST of your august, poetic race,

You go the last to your calm resting-place;

Yet though you pass from out our earthly view,

Your work remains, and Time shall give your due.

Whether beneath the tranquil Tuscan skies

You mused as all too soon the daylight dies,

Whether you watched from your far island home

The English Channel's eddying miles of foam,

Or whether in your mild declining days

You sojourned 'mid our London's clamorous ways,

Yours was the poet's life through length of years,

Yours were the poet's joys, and hopes, and fears;

Yours were the tender ministries of song,

Yours were the pleasures which to bards belong

Who, dwelling in the world, yet "dwell apart,"

And think but of their God and of their art.

Our gain from lives like yours no verse can tell:

Eldest of English poets, fare you well.

LONDON, *February* 26, 1898.

To a Lady playing the Harp
in her Chamber

(The Countess Rosalie von Sauerma-Zülzendorf,
niece of Spohr)

I

LADY, whose conscious fingers sweep the strings
    With all the true musician's living power,
I watch your hand, your gentle hand, which clings
    To that loved harp which has your touch for
        dower.
How perfect is your skill, the fruit of years —
    Years full of labour, years of patient thought!

Such tones as yours can move the heart to tears:

   With keen delight such tones as yours are

     fraught.

Now while the soft notes in their sweetness rise,

   Now while the wave of music dies away,

I seem to see the soul which lights your eyes —

   The soul which lends the magic while you play.

To Music's self how deep is your devotion;

Your strains are not mere Art — they are Emotion.

II

You told me once of that dear mother's love

   Whose goodness was the sunshine of your youth,

Whose smile "made paradise" for you, who strove

   To point the way to happy paths of Truth.

You told me how through Life's dark days of
    grief —
    Through all Life's dreary days of changeful
    care —
The thought of her fond love could bring relief,
    The thought of her fond love could quell
    despair.
And now I know that in your music's sweetness,
    In its most subtle power to move the heart,
In its true grandeur, in its rare completeness,
    Your mother's hallowed influence has a part —
An influence present yet and ceasing never,
An influence gathering strength and beauty ever.

RELIGIOUS POEMS

6

To Christina Rossetti

Great as a Poet, greater as a Woman

(Died December 29, 1894)

I MARVEL not that God hath called away

    Thy peerless soul to where His saints abide;

Rather I praise Him that He bade thee stay

    On earth so long — to be a heavenward guide.

A Sunrise in Early Summer

I

Now lagging black-browed Night at last is
  gone,

And fair and happy Dawn at length is here.

How sweet the sights which now I look upon —

The sights of summer beauty growing clear!

The meadows yonder and the lawn appear

Glittering with dewdrops — dewdrops silvery,
  white,

Touched by the sun's first beams; while far and
  near

Each bird, each flower awakes, and hails the
   sight
Of coming morn: to them like me it brings
   delight.

II

To eastward lies a mass of sable cloud
Made glorious by the rising sun, who flings
His rays athwart its depths.   I hear the loud
Yet mellow thrush's note — a blackbird sings
With sudden burst of song — a lark up-springs
From that wide field of wheat; so more and
   more
Sounds Nature's orchestra of myriad strings.
I watch the apple-bloom, while May-buds pour
On all the gentle air their matchless, fragrant
   store.

III

O, who at sunrise could be aught but glad —

Sunrise, the prototype of perfect day,

When we shall wake to bliss, nor weak nor sad,

And, feeling swiftly the seraphic ray

From God's effulgence, cast the fears away

Which still cleave to us, and with rapturous
  soul

Know that black Trouble can no longer stay

In His blest presence — know the precious goal

Where all Earth's grievous wounds are made for
  ever whole.

Her Boy Just Dead

(A Mother Speaks)

My darling dead! Is all the long endeavour

    To vanquish Death in vain? These wistful

    eyes,

So Truth-illumed and loving, will they never

    Check by a look again my futile sighs?

And shall I weep — although for him the gladness

    Of this world's many pleasures now is o'er,

And I am left with this my load of sadness,

    Which here on earth is mine for evermore?

A cripple's lot were his, had he, remaining,

  Here ta'en his part where grief and care are

  rife —

Little of sinless happiness obtaining,

  Feeling all miseries of earthly life.

To shorten that hard period of probation

  Given to such as he so often here —

To raise him soon to an immortal station

  Where comes no thoughtless word, no taunt,

  no jeer —

The Master, in His mercy, gently made him

  Fitter among His ransomed ones to be —

And day by day more perfectly arrayed him

  In His own peerless robe of purity.

Then shall I cherish an abiding sorrow

For him whom God in goodness calls away?

Nay, rather let me muse on that blest morrow

Which joins in bliss our severed souls for aye.

Miracles

CHRIST'S wondrous miracles were signs indeed

Of wondrous power; yet every miracle

Of His had moral purpose, and was wrought

To show this moral purpose: and perchance

Thus is it that no longer we possess

The power to do such deeds.   Had you or I

Such gifts, we still should heal unceasingly,

Nor judge of the effects were cures but made.

Where then would be God's discipline of pain?

Where His just government of all His world?

Where then would be His discipline of sorrow?

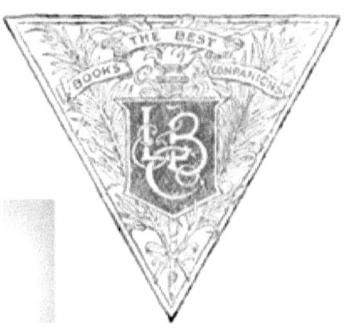

CHRISTINA ROSSETTI

A BIOGRAPHICAL AND CRITICAL STUDY

With Six Portraits and Six Facsimiles. $2.50.

Third Edition

QUEEN VICTORIA, in accepting a copy of this work, has expressed, through her secretary, Col. Sir Arthur Bigge, her thanks for the "interesting memoir."

" It is natural there should be a demand for a life of so true a poet as the late Christina Rossetti; she was such a beautiful character and made so deep an impression upon her friends, that any authentic record of her must be worth reading." — *Times, London.*

" Practically everything that anyone is entitled to know about the poetess is told us." — *Standard, London.*

" The author has had the advantage of personal knowledge and the encouragement of the surviving member of that gifted family. He has done all that a man could do for the theme." — *Daily Chronicle, London.*

" The volume fulfils its purpose excellently; the author is in full sympathy with his subject and, we should judge, has presented the poet to the world as she would have wished herself to be seen. . . . The portraits are delicately charming." — *Athenæum, London.*

" While claiming merely to have discharged the ' easier functions of an exponent,' Mr. Mackenzie Bell proves that he possesses the critical faculty in a very rare degree." — *Publishers' Circular, London (leader).*

CHARLES WHITEHEAD

A FORGOTTEN GENIUS

A Monograph

New Edition.   Cloth, 85 cents.

" It is strange how men with a true touch of genius in them can sink out of recognition. Mr. Mackenzie Bell's sketch may be welcomed for reviving the interest in Whitehead." — *Times, London.*

" Mr. Mackenzie Bell writes in an excellent style, and his critical remarks are full of thoughtful good sense." — *Contemporary Review, London.*

" This fascinating book. . . . Mr. Mackenzie Bell has done a peculiar service to letters." — *Daily News, London.*

" No fault can be found with the manner in which Mr. Mackenzie Bell has accomplished his difficult task. He had been inspired by an enthusiasm honourable to the biographer's sense of justice and deep, far-reaching sympathy." — *Morning Post, London.*

" His monograph is carefully, neatly, and sympathetically built up." — *Globe, London.*